WAR HISTORIES

THE VIETNAM WAR

BY ALEX MONROE

BELLWETHER MEDIA ★ MINNEAPOLIS, MN

Torque brims with excitement perfect for thrill-seekers of all kinds. Discover daring survival skills, explore uncharted worlds, and marvel at mighty engines and extreme sports. In *Torque* books, anything can happen. Are you ready?

This edition first published in 2024 by Bellwether Media, Inc.

No part of this publication may be reproduced in whole or in part without written permission of the publisher. For information regarding permission, write to Bellwether Media, Inc., Attention: Permissions Department, 6012 Blue Circle Drive, Minnetonka, MN 55343.

Library of Congress Cataloging-in-Publication Data

Names: Monroe, Alex (Writer of children's books), author.
Title: The Vietnam War / by Alex Monroe.
Description: Minneapolis, MN : Bellwether Media, Inc., 2024. | Series: Torque: war histories | Includes bibliographical references and index. | Audience: Ages 7-12 | Audience: Grades 4-6 | Summary: "Engaging images accompany information about the Vietnam War. The combination of high-interest subject matter and light text is intended for students in grades 3 through 7"– Provided by publisher.
Identifiers: LCCN 2023007743 (print) | LCCN 2023007744 (ebook) | ISBN 9798886874532 (library binding) | ISBN 9798886875454 (paperback) | ISBN 9798886876413 (ebook)
Subjects: LCSH: Vietnam War, 1961-1975–Juvenile literature.
Classification: LCC DS557.7 .M637 2024 (print) | LCC DS557.7 (ebook) | DDC 959.704/3–dc23/eng/20230221
LC record available at https://lccn.loc.gov/2023007743
LC ebook record available at https://lccn.loc.gov/2023007744

Text copyright © 2024 by Bellwether Media, Inc. TORQUE and associated logos are trademarks and/or registered trademarks of Bellwether Media, Inc.

Editor: Elizabeth Neuenfeldt   Designer: Josh Brink

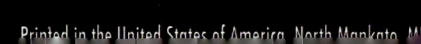

TABLE OF CONTENTS

WHAT WAS THE VIETNAM WAR?	4
THE PATH TO WAR	6
JOINING THE FIGHT	10
TURNING THE TIDE	14
THE IMPACT OF WAR	18
GLOSSARY	22
TO LEARN MORE	23
INDEX	24

WHAT WAS THE VIETNAM WAR?

The Vietnam War began in 1954. It ended in 1975. It was fought between North Vietnam and South Vietnam. Cambodia and Laos were also involved. The **Soviet Union** helped the North. The United States helped the South.

The war was fought over **communism**. The North supported it. The South did not. The war led to Vietnam becoming one country again in 1976.

VIETNAM WAR MAP

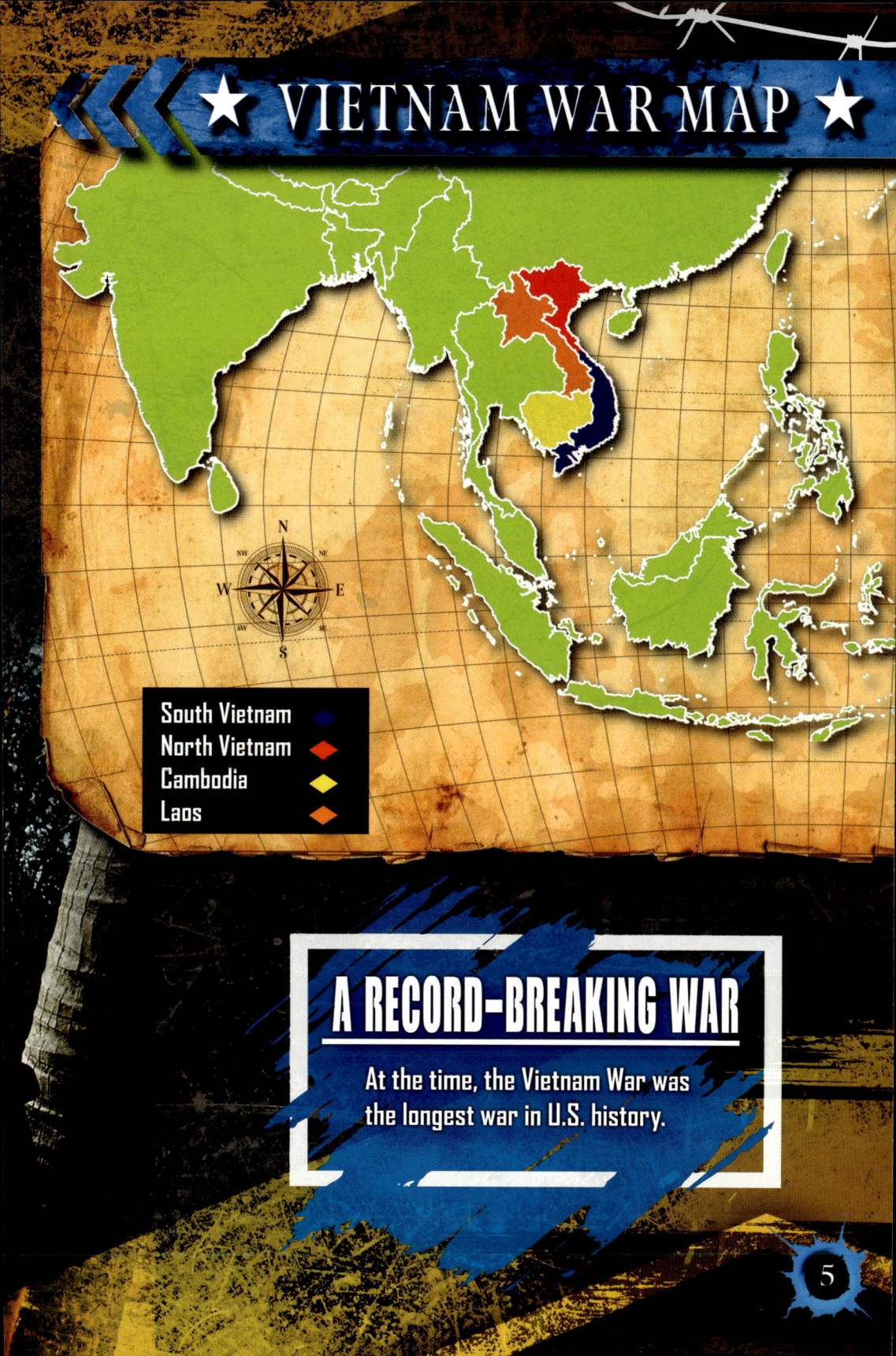

- South Vietnam
- North Vietnam
- Cambodia
- Laos

A RECORD-BREAKING WAR

At the time, the Vietnam War was the longest war in U.S. history.

THE PATH TO WAR

Starting in the 1800s, France controlled Vietnam. Ho Chi Minh worked to free Vietnam. In 1954, Vietnam won its freedom.

HO CHI MINH

Officials from many nations met. They split Vietnam into two countries. One was North Vietnam. The other was South Vietnam. Soon, both sides went to war over communism.

Meanwhile, the U.S. and the Soviet Union were enemies. They were in the Cold War. The Soviet Union wanted to spread communism. The U.S. wanted to stop it.

NORTH VIETNAMESE LEADER

NAME
Ho Chi Minh

NATIONALITY
Vietnamese

RANK
President of North Vietnam (1945 to 1969)

IMPORTANT ACTIONS
- 1945: Stated Vietnam was its own country

- 1954: Led Vietnamese forces to defeat France and win freedom

- 1954 to 1969: Led North Vietnam against South Vietnam

AMERICAN LEADER

NAME
Lyndon B. Johnson

NATIONALITY
American

RANK
President of the U.S. (1963 to 1969)

IMPORTANT ACTIONS
- 1964: Gained government support to act after the Gulf of Tonkin incident

- 1965: Ordered bombings in North Vietnam

- 1968: Paused U.S. bombing in North Vietnam to work toward peace

The U.S. and the Soviets did not fight each other directly. Instead, the U.S. helped South Vietnam. The Soviet Union helped the North. Both nations sent supplies and soldiers.

JOINING THE FIGHT

In August 1964, U.S. ships fought North Vietnamese forces. It happened in the Gulf of Tonkin.

USS *MADDOX* IN THE GULF OF TONKIN

WHAT'S IT CALLED?

The U.S. never officially declared war in Vietnam. The conflict there is sometimes called a "police action."

No one was certain if it was an attack. Some said the U.S. ships were not attacked. President Lyndon B. Johnson said they were. He wanted to take action. In March 1965, 3,500 U.S. troops arrived in South Vietnam.

Each side fought in its own way. The **Vietcong** fought for North Vietnam. Its members used **guerrilla warfare**. They dressed like **civilians**. They were hard to find.

The U.S. attacked where they thought the Vietcong hid. They dropped bombs and **herbicides** in jungles. They destroyed farms and villages with fire. Many Vietnamese civilians were killed.

SOLDIERS IN THE VIETNAM WAR

Vietcong
- dressed like civilians
- attacked with mines and traps
- sneaked up on enemies in jungles

U.S. Soldiers
- wore uniforms
- attacked with bombs and fire
- went on patrols to draw out enemies

TURNING THE TIDE

The U.S. **drafted** men to fight. By 1967, nearly 500,000 U.S. troops were in Vietnam. Many troops had already died.

In the U.S., many leaders said the U.S. was winning the war. Some Americans disagreed. They thought too many people were dying. People **protested** the war and the draft.

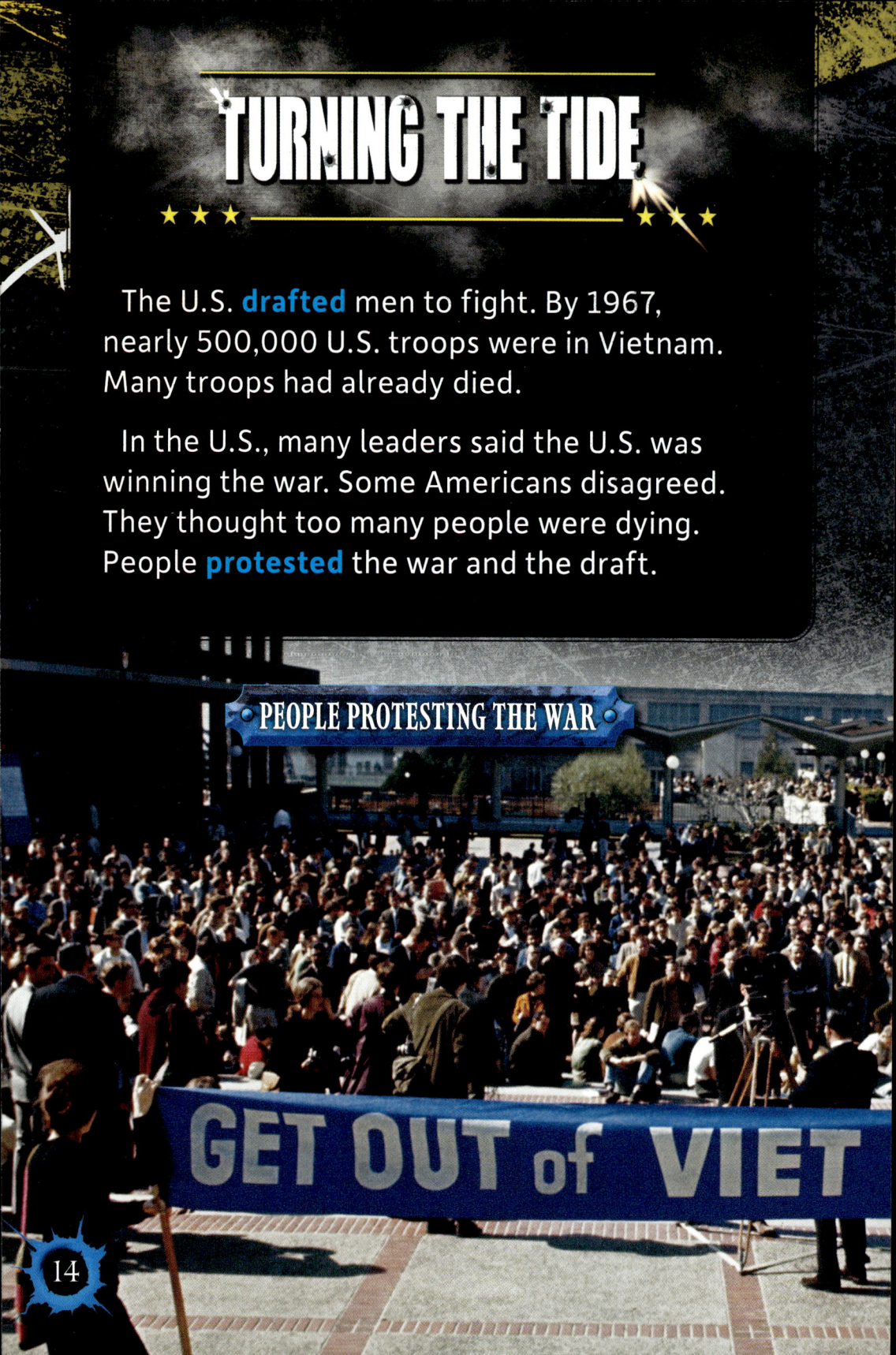

PEOPLE PROTESTING THE WAR

THE WAR AT HOME

The war cost the U.S. government a lot of money. The prices of goods rose in the U.S.

Many Americans had TVs in their homes. They watched daily news reports about the war. Some viewers felt angry about what they saw. People protested against the war. They marched and wrote songs.

AN UNFAIR DRAFT

Most people drafted into Vietnam were poor. Black Americans were more likely to be drafted than white Americans. Many Americans thought this was unfair.

On January 31, 1968, North Vietnamese fighters made a big attack. It was called the **Tet Offensive**. For weeks, they struck many cities in the South.

The attack shocked many Americans. They had believed North Vietnam was losing the war. The Tet Offensive showed that the North was still strong. Many people lost trust in U.S. leaders. Protests in the U.S. grew.

THE IMPACT OF WAR

U.S. leaders saw that they could not win the war. In March 1973, the last U.S. troops left Vietnam. North and South Vietnam continued to fight.

In 1975, North Vietnam won the war. In 1976, the two sides became one nation. It was called the Socialist Republic of Vietnam.

VIETNAM WAR TIMELINE

1954
Vietnam is split into North and South Vietnam

August 1964
The Gulf of Tonkin incident occurs

March 1965
The first U.S. combat troops arrive in Vietnam

January 31, 1968
The Tet Offensive begins

1973
The last U.S. troops leave Vietnam

1975
North Vietnam wins the war

1976
The Socialist Republic of Vietnam forms

The war destroyed farms and villages in Vietnam. There were many **casualties**. Over one million Vietnamese people became **refugees**. Many Americans lost trust in their leaders. **Veterans** were sometimes treated poorly. Today, **memorials** honor those who served.

Many were affected by the Vietnam War. It took many years for the U.S. and Vietnam to begin working together. The war's impact still continues today.

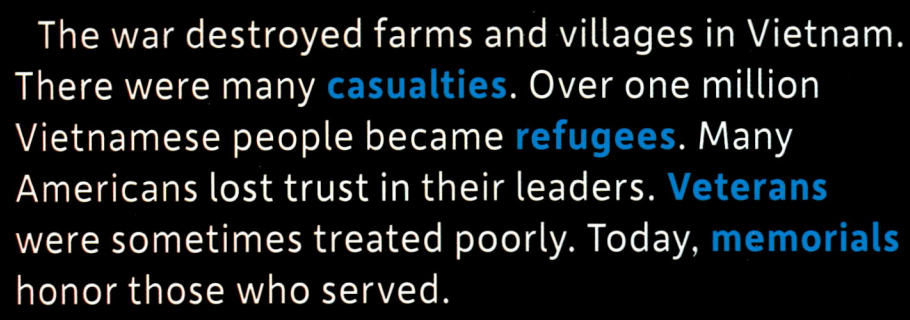

VIETNAM VETERANS MEMORIAL IN WASHINGTON, D.C.

BY THE NUMBERS

10,000 U.S. soldiers = 10,000 Vietcong and North Vietnamese soldiers = 10,000 South Vietnamese soldiers = 10,000 civilians =

MAIN COUNTRIES INVOLVED

- Cambodia, China, Laos, North Vietnam, South Korea, South Vietnam, Soviet Union, United States

ESTIMATED DEATHS

- North Vietnam and Vietcong: around 1,100,000 soldiers

- South Vietnam: up to 250,000 soldiers

- U.S.: 58,220 soldiers

- Civilian deaths (North and South Vietnam): around 2,000,000 people

U.S. STATE WITH THE MOST CASUALTIES

- California 5,572

TOTAL U.S. MILITARY PERSONNEL SENT TO VIETNAM

- about 2,700,000

COST OF THE WAR TO THE U.S.

- around $111 billion ($974 billion today)

GLOSSARY

casualties—war-related deaths and injuries combined

civilians—people who are not part of the armed forces

Cold War—a conflict between the U.S. and the Soviet Union in the second half of the 1900s that did not break out into fighting

communism—a social system in which property is controlled by the government

drafted—selected men who would be required to fight in the armed forces

guerrilla warfare—a type of military combat that involves surprise attacks and quick conflicts instead of traditional battles

herbicides—chemicals intended to kill plants; herbicides are poisonous to humans.

memorials—places that serve as reminders of events or people

protested—gathered in public groups to object to the war

refugees—people forced to flee their country or home because of war or other disasters

Soviet Union—a country in eastern Europe and western Asia that existed from 1922 to 1991

Tet Offensive—a series of North Vietnamese attacks on many cities in South Vietnam from January 31 to March 28, 1968

veterans—people who have served in the military

Vietcong—Vietnamese communist guerrilla fighters

TO LEARN MORE

AT THE LIBRARY

Markovics, Joyce. *1969 Vietnam War Protest March*. Ann Arbor, Mich.: Cherry Lake Publishing, 2021.

Murray, Stuart. *Vietnam War*. New York, N.Y.: DK, 2017.

O'Connor, Jim. *What Was the Vietnam War?* New York, N.Y.: Penguin Workshop, 2019.

ON THE WEB

FACTSURFER

Factsurfer.com gives you a safe, fun way to find more information.

1. Go to www.factsurfer.com

2. Enter "Vietnam War" into the search box and click 🔍.

3. Select your book cover to see a list of related content.

INDEX

Black Americans, 15
by the numbers, 21
Cambodia, 4, 5
casualties, 20
civilians, 12
Cold War, 8
communism, 4, 7, 8
draft, 14, 15
France, 6
guerilla warfare, 12
Gulf of Tonkin, 10, 11
Johnson, Lyndon B., 9, 11
Laos, 4, 5
leaders, 8, 9
map, 5, 17
memorials, 20
Minh, Ho Chi, 6, 8
North Vietnam, 4, 5, 7, 9, 10, 12, 16, 18

police action, 11
protests, 14, 15, 16
refugees, 20
Socialist Republic of Vietnam, 18
soldiers, 9, 13
South Vietnam, 4, 5, 7, 9, 11, 16, 18
Soviet Union, 4, 8, 9
supplies, 9
Tet Offensive, 16, 17
timeline, 18–19
troops, 11, 14, 18
United States, 4, 5, 8, 9, 10, 11, 12, 13, 14, 16, 18, 20
veterans, 20
Vietcong, 12, 13
war at home, 15

The images in this book are reproduced through the courtesy of: Wirestock Creators, cover (explosion); James K. F. Dung, SFC/ Wiki Commons, cover (helicopters & troops), pp. 2-3, 22-23, 24; Robin Kay, cover (background); Dominique BERRETTY/ Getty Images, pp. 4-5; RBM Vintage Images/ Alamy, p. 6; Pictures From History/ Alamy, pp. 6-7, 18 (1964 entry); World History Archive/ Alamy, p. 8; Arnold Newman, White House Press Office/ Wiki Commons, pp. 8-9; U.S. Navy photo/ Wiki Commons, pp. 10-11; PJF Military Collection/ Alamy, p. 11; manhhai, pp. 12-13; Corbis Historical/ Getty Images, pp. 14-15; Bettmann/ Getty Images, p. 15; Archive Photos/ Getty Images, pp. 16-17; ASSOCIATED PRESS/ AP News Room, pp. 18-19; US military personnel/ Wiki Commons, p. 19 (1968 entry); Sean Pavone, pp. 20-21; SSG Howard C. Breedlove/ Wiki Commons, back cover.